To the Rescue

by Monica Hughes

DENNIS
N182 SDA

Editorial consultant: Mitch Cronick

Copyright © **ticktock Entertainment Ltd 2006**
First published in Great Britain in 2006 by **ticktock Media Ltd.,**
Unit 2, Orchard Business Centre, North Farm Road, Tunbridge Wells, Kent TN2 3XF

We would like to thank: Shirley Bickler and Suzanne Baker

ISBN 1 86007 970 9 pbk
Printed in China

Picture credits
t=top, b=bottom, c=centre, l-left, r=right, OFC= outside front cover
Corbis: 16-17. Freefoto: OFC, 8. Oshkosh: 12-13. Shutterstock: 9b, 10, 20.
Superstock: 5, 6-7, 10-11, 18, 19. ticktock photography: 4, 14-15.
US Coastguard: 17, 21.

CONTENTS

Ambulance 4

Police 6

Fire engines 8

Fighting fires 10

Airport fire 12

Forest fire 14

Fireboat 16

Snow plough 18

Helicopters 20

Talking about rescue vehicles 22

Activities 24

Ambulance

An ambulance goes to help people who are hurt or ill.

The blue lights flash.

Blue lights

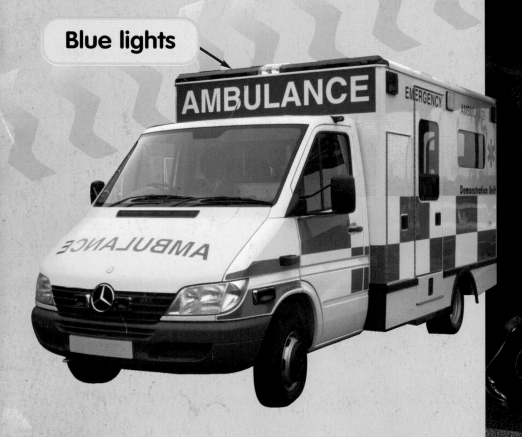

The siren goes off.

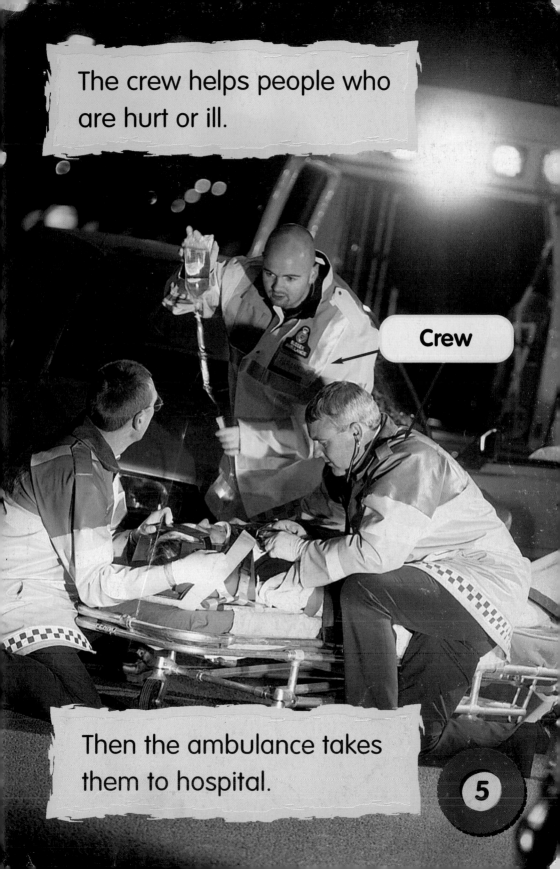

The crew helps people who are hurt or ill.

Crew

Then the ambulance takes them to hospital.

5

Police

There is a big accident.

The police go to help.

The police have fast cars.

Flashing lights

The police have fast
motorbikes too.

The cars have a siren
and lights that flash.

Fire engines

There is a big fire.

The fire engine goes to help.

Blue lights

The blue lights flash.

Some fire engines have long ladders.

Ladders

The ladders lift the firefighters up high.

Fighting fires

The fire engine has long hoses.

Hoses

The firefighters spray water on the fire.

The water puts the fire out.

Airport fire

There is a fire at the airport.

The Striker goes to help.

The Striker is a giant fire engine.

It sprays foam on the fire.

The foam puts the fire out.

Forest fire

There is a fire in a forest.

The airtanker flies over the forest.

Forest Fire

It drops powder on the fire.

The powder puts the fire out.

15

Fireboat

The fireboat puts out fires at sea and on rivers.

It sprays water on the fire.

It gets the water from the sea or the river.

LOS ANGELES FIRE DEPARTMENT

DANGER ● PROPELLERS

17

Snow plough

This road is blocked by snow.

Cars cannot get past.

The snow plough
comes to the rescue.

The snow plough can push the snow away.

Now the cars can pass.

19

Helicopters

Helicopters can help people.

This helicopter goes to help people who are hurt or ill.

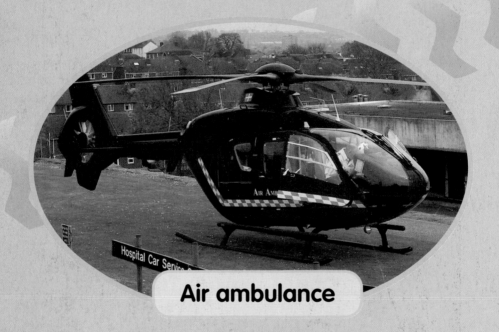

Air ambulance

It takes them to hospital.

It is called an air ambulance.

This helicopter can rescue someone who is in the sea.

The crew pull the person up on a rope.

Talking about rescue vehicles

What has got ladders and hoses?

- **a police car**
- **an airtanker**
- **a fire engine**

Which has got a siren?

- **an ambulance**
- **a police car**
- **a snow plough**

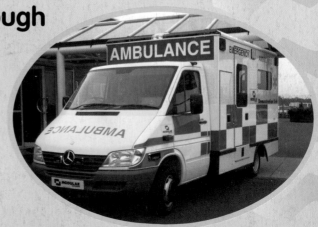

Where does the Striker
fight fires?

- **in a forest**
- **at sea**
- **at an airport**

What does an
airtanker drop?

- **water**
- **powder**
- **foam**

Which rescue would
you like to help with?
Why?

Activities

What did you think of this book?

 Brilliant   **Good**    **OK**

Which page did you like best? Why?

• • • • • • • • • • • • • • •

Which is the odd one out? Why?

airtanker • fireboat • helicopter

• • • • • • • • • • • • •

Draw a big picture of a fire engine and label it. Use these words:

hose • ladder • lights

• • • • • • • • • • • • •

Who is the author of this book?
Have you read *Busy Trucks* by the same author?

24